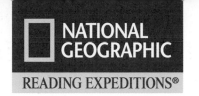

## NATIONAL GEOGRAPHIC
### READING EXPEDITIONS®

EYEWITNESS

# The Tri-State Tornado

By Rebecca L. Johnson
Illustrated by Ken Call

Produced through the worldwide resources of
the National Geographic Society, John M.
Fahey, Jr., President and Chief Executive
Officer; Gilbert M. Grosvenor, Chairman of the
Board; Nina D. Hoffman, Executive Vice
President and President, Books and Education
Publishing Group.

**Prepared by National Geographic School
Publishing**
Ericka Markman, Senior Vice President and
President, Children's Books and Education
Publishing Group; Steve Mico, Senior Vice
President, Publisher, Editorial Director; Francis
Downey, Executive Editor; Richard Easby,
Editorial Manager; Bea Jackson, Director of
Design; Cindy Olson, Art Director; Margaret
Sidlosky, Director of Illustrations; Matt
Wascavage, Manager of Publishing Services;
Lisa Pergolizzi, Sean Philpotts, Production
Managers; Ted Tucker, Production Specialist.

**Manufacturing and Quality Control**
Christopher A. Liedel, Chief Financial Officer;
Phillip L. Schlosser, Director; Clifton M. Brown,
Manager.

**Editors**
Barbara Seeber, Mary Anne Wengel

**Book Development**
Morrison BookWorks LLC

**Book Design**
Steven Curtis Design

**Art Direction**
Dan Banks, Project Design Company

Published by the National Geographic Society
1145 17th Street, N.W.
Washington, D.C. 20036-4688

ISBN: 0-7922-5865-7

2010  2009  2008  2007  2006
1 2 3 4 5 6 7 8 9 10 11 12 13 14 15

# CONTENTS

# Murphysboro, Illinois

 SOUTHERN ILLINOIS is mostly an area of flatland that is good for farming. There are many small towns that are separated by large areas of farmland. Murphysboro is one of these small farming communities. The location of Murphysboro, the flat land, and the warm climate in the spring and summer create conditions that are perfect for severe storms that sometimes lead to tornados. In southern Illinois, these storms rarely occur in the springtime.

On a spring day in 1925, no one in the town of Murphysboro had any reason to think a tornado could happen.

▲ Downtown Murphysboro in 1910

▲ Southern Illinois has miles of flat farmland.

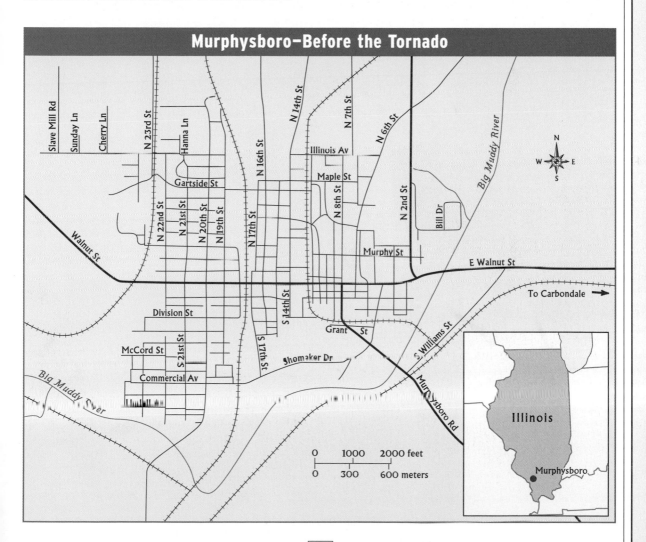

**Murphysboro–Before the Tornado**

Slave Mill Rd
Sunday Ln
Cherry Ln
N 23rd St
Hanna Ln
N 14th St
N 7th St
N 6th St
Illinois Av
Big Muddy River
N
W · E
S
Maple St
Gartside St
N 16th St
N 8th St
N 2nd St
N 22nd St
N 21st St
N 20th St
N 19th St
N 17th St
Bill Dr
Murphy St
Walnut St
E Walnut St
To Carbondale →
Division St
S 14th St
McCord St
S 21st St
S 17th St
Grant St
S Williams St
Shomaker Dr
Commercial Av
Big Muddy River
Murphysboro Rd

0    1000    2000 feet
0    300    600 meters

Illinois

Murphysboro

# CHAPTER 1

# Murphysboro

MATTIE DUNN slipped her hand gently under the white-feathered hen. Annoyed, the bird raised itself up off its nest and clucked loudly. "Oh, calm down," shushed Mattie, grabbing the two warm eggs that lay nestled in the cup of straw. She stroked the hen until it settled back on its nest.

Mattie put the eggs gently in the bottom of the old wicker basket. "Two, four, six, eight . . . nine," she whispered softly to herself, counting the eggs. Mattie crossed to the other side of the chicken house, padding softly over the layer of fresh straw that covered the floor. The straw smelled sweet. Dust particles danced in the sunbeams that angled through the spaces between the old boards of the wall.

From the barn, Mattie heard a gentle *moooo* and the clanking of a milk pail. Her brother, Henry, was milking Bessie, the Dunn's milk cow. A rooster crowed out in the yard, and from off in the distance came the lowing of the cattle in the pasture. Mattie loved this time of day, after the sun had just risen and everything was waking up from a long night's sleep.

Mattie found more eggs in the remaining nests. That made 14 in all. Her mother would be pleased. Mattie pushed open the rickety door of the chicken house and stepped out into the early morning air. Sunlight was glinting off the blades of the windmill. Mattie closed the door behind her. Then she headed for the barn, picking her way around the worst patches of mud. The ground was thawing. Grass was greening up all over the yard. The air felt heavy and moist. It was March 17, a time when snow was usually still on the ground in southern Illinois. But spring seemed to be early this year.

The big barn door was open. Mattie stepped into the barn's cool shadows. Her brother was seated on a wooden stool, with his head pressed against the side of the big black-and-white cow. As Henry milked the cow, jets of milk squirted into a pail. Half a dozen cats moved around Henry as he worked, rubbing up against his legs. They were hoping for a breakfast drink of warm milk.

"'Bout done?" Mattie asked her brother. Henry was 11, just one year younger than Mattie. But they were almost the same height. They both had dark brown hair and hazel-colored eyes.

"Almost," Henry replied.

Mattie moved farther into the barn, past the wagon and a neat stack of hay bales. Charger whinnied quietly as she walked up to his stall. The dappled gray horse tossed his head and ambled over to her. Mattie leaned across the gate and stroked his velvety soft nose. "And how are you this morning, boy?" she murmured softly. Charger pricked up his ears and swished his tail in response.

"OK, all done," Henry called out. He set the pail of warm, frothy milk carefully to one side. He hung up the milking stool and led Bessie back to her stall. "Come on, Sis!" he urged, picking up the pail. "I'm starving!" Mattie followed behind him with the basket of eggs.

Chickens scattered in front of them as they hurried across the yard toward the house. It was a white, two-story house with green shutters and a long front porch. The paint on the clapboard siding was peeling here and there. Beyond the house was a dense grove of trees that blocked the view of the road that ran past the farm.

As Mattie and Henry trotted up the steps to the front porch, their mother pushed open the screen door and stepped out.

"Perfect timing, you two!" Stella Dunn exclaimed, smiling and pushing a wave of mahogany-colored hair back from her face. "I was just about to call you in for breakfast." She took the pail of milk and basket of eggs.

Henry and Mattie slipped off their overshoes and hurried into the warm kitchen.

The buttery aroma of biscuits filled the room. At the sink, William Dunn, dressed in overalls and a red plaid shirt, was washing his hands. "Morning, kids," he said smiling. He wiped his hands on a towel and sank down into a chair at the kitchen table.

Mattie's mother took a tray of hot golden biscuits out of the oven. "I declare," she said, "it really does feel like spring today."

"Well, if this weather holds," William responded, "then the spring of 1925 will be the earliest spring I can remember!" He paused, taking the plate of biscuits smothered with sausage gravy that his wife handed him. "Maybe this will be the year we've been waiting for, Stella. Maybe we will get that bumper crop that will help us get out of debt."

Mattie watched her mother smile cautiously. As long as she could remember, her parents had struggled to make ends meet on the farm. The cattle and crops her parents raised and sold every year earned just enough money to pay the mortgage and keep things going on the farm. There was rarely money left after all the necessities had been taken care of, especially for such things as toys or store-bought clothes.

"Mattie," her mother said, trying to change the subject. "I mended your brown dress last night, so you can wear it to school today."

"Oh." Mattie's shoulders sagged. She paused and then plunged ahead, "I was hoping I could wear my yellow dress to school today."

"Oh, Mattie," her mother sighed. "You know that dress is only for special occasions. Your brown dress is just fine for school."

Mattie broke off a piece of biscuit with her fork and pushed it across her plate. She hated her brown dress. It had been mended many times. The edge of the collar was fraying. She wanted so badly to have something new and fine to wear to school.

"Maybe . . . " Mattie hesitated. " . . . Maybe if we get a good crop this year, I can get some new dresses for school—at Blakewell's Dress Shop in town."

Her parents stopped eating and glanced at each other. Mattie's father cleared his throat. "Mattie," he said gently, "pretty clothes are not as important as food and seed and all the other things we need. Blakewell's has the most expensive clothes in Murphysboro. Don't go getting your heart set on fine things, honey. They're not important."

Mattie stared down at her plate. For a moment, she considered telling her father what was happening at school. Maybe then he would understand why nice things were important. But before she could even think of where to begin, her mother spoke up.

"Hurry up now," she urged. "Finish your breakfast and get dressed for school."

As Henry downed the rest of his milk, Mattie cleared their plates and hurried upstairs to her room. She opened the door of her wardrobe and stared at the clothes hanging there. Except for her yellow dress with its cream-colored lace, everything looked old and drab. Mattie sighed and turned to the bed where her mother had laid out her brown dress. She slipped off her shirt and

**dungarees** and put on the dress. Then she looked at her reflection in the mirror on the wardrobe door. She sighed again, hating the brown dress more than ever.

Downstairs, Mattie's mother handed Mattie and her brother their tin lunch pails. They kissed her goodbye and went out. Their father was at the bottom of the porch steps, lacing up his boots. He was going out into the fields to see whether the ground had thawed enough to start plowing.

"Bye, Pop!" Henry cried, punching his father playfully in the arm.

William Dunn ruffled his son's dark hair. "If it's too wet to plow, Henry," he said, "I'm going to fix the doors on the storm cellar. Several boards need replacing, and the hinges are rusted. If I'm not finished by the time you get home from school, you can give me a hand."

"Sure," said Henry.

Mattie remembered last summer's big thunderstorm that had sent them all running for cover in the storm cellar. Her father had thought the storm might spawn a tornado. But it had just rained hard and hailed. Mattie had never seen a tornado. But both her parents had. Their descriptions of a tornado's whirling funnel cloud always gave her goose bumps.

---

**dungarees** – pants or overalls made of a heavy, durable cotton, such as denim

"Is this tornado weather, Dad?" Mattie asked.

"Not really, Mattie," he replied. "Bad storms, like tornadoes, usually come in the summertime. But fixing the storm cellar is a job that needs doing, and today is as good as any."

Mattie's father looked up at his daughter. "You look especially pretty today," he said. Mattie tried to smile. But her heart wasn't in it. She wasn't feeling pretty at all in her old brown dress.

Mattie and Henry walked down the long drive that led from the house to the road. They could see the school bus coming. It rumbled up slowly and sputtered to a stop. Mattie and Henry stepped up inside and took seats near the front. Henry turned to talk to some of his friends across the aisle. But Mattie just stared out the window. She didn't feel like talking.

Leaves were budding on the trees that lined the road. The rolling hills that stretched to the horizon were tinged with the first bright greens of spring. After a few minutes, Mattie could see the town of Murphysboro through the windshield of the bus. The Dunn farm was only two miles from the town. A dozen miles beyond Murphysboro was the wide Mississippi River and the state of Missouri.

People in the area said Murphysboro was a town "on the go." Home to several thousand people, Murphysboro was a mix of busy streets and quiet neighborhoods. The town was on the railroad lines and had several factories. It also had several schools, a few churches, and many small stores.

The bus slowed and turned onto Main Street. Mattie pressed her face to the glass. There it was: Blakewell's Dress Shop. On the dark green awning, the words "Fine Designs for Ladies and Girls" were lettered in white. Mattie stared at the brightly colored dresses and shoes and hats displayed in the window. She craned her head as the bus moved past. There was something new in the window— a girl's dark blue dress with a white sash.

The dress and the shop disappeared as the school bus turned the corner. After a few more turns, the bus pulled in front of the school. Henry leaped out of his seat. Mattie got up reluctantly. She was the last one off the bus.

Hugging her schoolbooks and lunch pail to her chest, Mattie walked slowly across the schoolyard. Her school was a square two-story brick building with the main entrance right in the middle. The schoolyard was noisy and **chaotic** as dozens of students milled around in the warm sunshine, waiting for the bell to ring. Boys were playing tag and kickball. Some of the younger girls were playing hopscotch and jacks. But most of the girls in Mattie's class were standing around in small groups, talking among themselves.

Mattie heard Amanda Blakewell's laugh before she saw her. It was high and shrill and ended in a kind of snicker. And, as usual, Amanda was laughing at Mattie.

"Well, Mattie Dunn," Amanda sneered, stepping directly in front of Mattie. The girls who were clustered around Amanda giggled.

Mattie stopped dead in her tracks. She stared silently at Amanda, dreading what she knew was coming.

With her hands on her hips, Amanda began to circle Mattie slowly, looking her up and down.

Amanda was a pretty girl—maybe the prettiest girl in the whole school. She had china-blue eyes and long blonde hair. Today her hair was curled into bouncing ringlets tied with satin ribbons. The ribbons were pale green. They matched the pale green trim on Amanda's dress. It was a new dress, of course. Amanda often had new dresses.

---

**chaotic** – confused and disorganized

The Blakewells were very well-to-do. Amanda's father was a banker. Her mother owned Blakewell's Dress Shop. And she dressed her daughter in the best clothes from her shop. Amanda's parents gave her everything she wanted.

Amanda stopped in front of Mattie again, having made a complete circle around her. "It's the brown dress again," Amanda said, "the one you tore last week at recess." She peered at the hem where Mattie's mother had mended the tear. "Nice mending job," Amanda said, tilting her head so her ringlets bounced. "That must be your mother's work."

Mattie had been clenching her jaw so hard that her teeth hurt. She knew better than to say anything. But now she couldn't help it. "Don't make fun of my mother," she hissed at Amanda.

"Oh, Mattie," Amanda replied, smiling, revealing her perfectly white teeth. "I'm not making fun of your mother." She paused, glancing back at her friends. As she turned back to Mattie, her smile disappeared. "I'm making fun of you." Amanda and her friends all burst out laughing.

Mattie could feel her face burning. Finally, the school bell rang. Amanda turned on her heel and linked arms with two of her friends. Laughing, they headed for the door.

Mattie stood as if she were rooted to the ground. She hated her old brown dress. But she hated Amanda Blakewell even more.

# CHAPTER 2

# The Black Cloud

EARLY THE NEXT MORNING, Mattie woke up with a start. She'd been dreaming about school again—and Amanda. Mattie lay beneath the blanket, wishing it were Saturday, even wishing she were sick. The thought of going to school almost made her sick.

The trouble had started about a month ago. Before then, Amanda had hardly spoken to Mattie. Amanda typically ignored anyone who lived outside the town of Murphysboro—the farm kids, as she called them.

But one afternoon last month, everything had changed. When their teacher, Mrs. Patterson, had asked for a volunteer to help her put up a new bulletin board after school, Mattie had quickly raised her hand. So had Amanda. When Mrs. Patterson had chosen Mattie, Mattie was elated—until she saw the look on Amanda Blakewell's face. With narrowed eyes and an angry frown, Amanda had stared at her for a long time.

Mattie thought it would end there. But it didn't. The next day, Amanda had begun making fun of Mattie. She made nasty remarks about Mattie's straight hair and the fact that she lived "out with the cows" and rode the bus to school. Mattie had tried to ignore her. But then, when Amanda made fun of Mattie's clothes, Mattie had gotten angry. Amanda knew right then that she'd found Mattie's weak spot. After that, Amanda was relentless. She began to make fun of Mattie because she wore the same few dresses every week and her dresses were old and worn.

Mattie had told Henry about what Amanda was doing. He'd shrugged his shoulders and told her not to let it bother her. But it did. Mattie thought about telling her parents, but she knew they'd tell her the same thing. She worried that her mother might also go to talk with Mrs. Blakewell. That would be the worst thing that could happen. It would just make Amanda more determined to make Mattie's life miserable.

Mattie kept hoping that Amanda would eventually get tired of tormenting her. But it had been over a month, and Amanda showed no signs of stopping. Mattie didn't really know what to do.

Outside in the yard, a rooster crowed. Sighing, Mattie threw back the covers and got up to do her morning chores. An hour later, she and Henry were standing by the road, waiting for the school bus again.

Mattie glanced up at the sky, where low clouds hung like a curtain over the sun. It was a gloomy day, one that matched the way Mattie felt. A raindrop landed on her upturned face. Then another and another. But it was too warm to put on the raincoat she had brought along. It felt like June instead of March. The warm air was humid and absolutely still. Not a leaf stirred on the trees.

Mattie watched the bus pull up. Henry jumped up inside, but for a few seconds Mattie just stood there on the gravel. "Come on, Mattie!" said Henry. "What are you waiting for?"

Mattie slowly climbed the steps into the bus and took a seat. Ten minutes later, the bus pulled up in front of the school. As the other children filed off the bus, Mattie scanned the schoolyard for Amanda. When she spotted her, Mattie felt a sudden twinge of jealously. Amanda was wearing the dress that had been in the shop window the day before, the one with the white sash.

Henry was standing beside her. They were the last two children on the bus. Henry followed his sister's gaze and saw Amanda.

"Is Amanda still making fun of you, Mattie?" he asked softly.

"Yes," was all Mattie could manage to say.

"Aw, she's spoiled and stuck-up," he said. "Nobody really likes her. Why can't you just ignore her?" he asked.

"I don't know," Mattie replied. "I just can't seem to."

A mischievous smile spread slowly across Henry's face. "I could put a frog in her lunch pail."

Mattie laughed. "Thanks, Henry," she said, "but I don't think that would really help."

"Well, keep it in mind," Henry said as he headed toward the door. He hopped down onto the sidewalk and ran off. Mattie got off the bus slowly, much to the irritation of the bus driver. Seeing one of her friends, she hurried across the schoolyard toward her—and away from Amanda Blakewell.

The morning seemed to crawl by. Mattie had a hard time paying attention to Mrs. Patterson and the lessons. She noticed Amanda staring at her while the class was working math problems. As soon as she knew Mattie was watching, Amanda leaned forward and poked her friend Betsy seated in front of her. Amanda whispered something and pointed at Mattie's shoes. The two girls giggled so loudly that Mrs. Patterson looked up from her desk and gave them a stern look.

Mattie's classroom was on the second floor. It had big windows that looked out over the schoolyard and the houses across the street. It was so warm outside that Mrs. Patterson had opened all the windows. Mattie stared out the window closest to her desk. She noticed the sky was a dark mass of gray cloud. Every now and then, a sudden shower of raindrops would splatter on the windowsills. They fell straight down out of the sky because there still wasn't a breath of wind.

Lunch came and went and the afternoon classes began. At half past one, Mattie looked up from the history book she was reading and glanced outside. The sky was much darker now, especially in the southwest. It looked as though it was going to rain hard pretty soon.

"Mattie, please pay attention to your reading!" Mrs. Patterson's voice startled Mattie. Embarrassed, she turned back to her book. But moments later she noticed that Mrs. Patterson had gotten up from her desk and walked over to the windows. She was frowning. Mattie looked out at the sky. The dark cloud she'd seen before in the southwest had gotten much bigger and looked much closer now.

There was a soft tap at the classroom door. Every head turned as the door opened, and the principal stepped into the room. Mrs. Patterson hurried over. She and the principal spoke briefly in hushed whispers. Then the principal left, and Mrs. Patterson turned to the class and asked for everyone's attention.

"In a few minutes the bell will ring for recess," she said. "But as you can see, it's looking like rain. So don't be surprised if we cut recess short." She laughed somewhat nervously. "We don't want those of you without raincoats to get wet."

When the bell rang, Mattie and the other students filed out of the building. The warm air felt strangely heavy. All during recess, the sky grew darker and darker. Mattie walked around the schoolyard looking for Henry. She found him playing catch.

"Big storm coming, Sis," he said, catching the ball. "Maybe there'll be thunder and lightning!"

Mattie crossed her arms and hugged them tightly to her chest. She didn't like storms.

On the school's front steps, Mattie noticed that the teachers and the principal were pointing at the sky and talking among themselves. At 2:20, the bell rang unexpectedly, and the teachers began rounding up the students, urging them back inside. Some children groaned and complained about having their playtime cut short.

Back in the classroom, Mattie and her classmates lined up along the windows. The black cloud was absolutely huge now. As Mattie watched, she could actually see it approaching the town.

"Looks like it's going to be a real gully washer," someone said.

"Well, I just hope it isn't raining when we are dismissed," Amanda declared loudly. "I don't want to get my new dress wet."

Mattie rolled her eyes. She glanced up at the clock. It was 2:35. In one more hour she could get away from Amanda.

"Hey, look at that horse," someone else said. In the street outside the school, a horse-drawn cart was going by. The man driving it was having a terrible time. The horse was rearing up and pawing the air. The man tugged hard on the reins. But the horse paid no attention. It suddenly bolted and went tearing down the street while the man in the cart hung on for dear life.

"Everyone, take your seats, please!" Mrs. Patterson called out. Her voice was high and tense.

Reluctantly, the students returned to their desks. But they couldn't take their eyes off what was happening to the sky. In just a minute or two, the enormous black cloud had moved in to hang directly over Murphysboro. It was the biggest, blackest cloud Mattie had ever seen. It looked like it was rolling over and over, like a barrel rolling through the sky. And it was moving very fast.

As the cloud settled over Murphysboro, a strange smoky fog began to move rapidly through the town. At the same time, the wind began to blow. All day the air had been eerily still. Now a huge gust of wind slammed into the school. Grit and dust billowed in through the open windows. The glass rattled in the window frames.

Mrs. Patterson rushed over to shut the windows as quickly as she could. "Stay in your seats, everyone!" she shouted. Mattie could hear fear in her teacher's voice.

Suddenly the lights went out, plunging the classroom into deep shadows. Outside it was now almost as dark as night. It was as if a giant dark monster were looming over Murphysboro, blocking out the light. For a split second Mrs. Patterson stood motionless, transfixed by the scene outside the windows. Mattie followed her gaze and felt a strange twisting in her stomach.

The cloud was no longer just a rolling mass of blackness. Mattie could see things moving around inside it: telegraph poles, signs, tree limbs. A thousand things were soaring through the sky above the city. And it was all moving toward the school faster than a train racing down the tracks.

Mrs. Patterson spun around and faced the class. "Everyone! Listen to me! Move quickly into the hallway." She began herding children in front of her toward the classroom door. Mattie leaped to her feet. Children around her began to push and shove as panic spread through the room.

Something blew against one of the windows and the glass cracked with a sound like a rifle shot.

"Hurry, children! Hurry!" Mrs. Patterson cried. "Get into the hall! Crouch down! Cover your heads with your arms!"

Mattie was almost to the door. Someone pushed from behind, almost knocking her down. She grabbed the door frame and squeezed through. The hallway was very dark and crowded with children from other classes. Instinctively, Mattie turned left toward Henry's classroom, which was just one room down from hers.

"Henry!" Mattie called out, searching the shadows for her brother's face. She saw him standing a few feet away, in the middle of the hall next to the railing that ran around the top of the stairwell.

"Henry!" she called again. This time Henry heard her. Mattie saw her brother open his mouth to reply. But she never heard his response. At that moment all the windows in the classroom behind her exploded.

# CHAPTER 3

# A Roaring, Whirling Nightmare

EVERYTHING HAPPENED at once. Razor-sharp shards of glass shot into the hallway. Children screamed and covered their faces. Mrs. Patterson, who had been standing in the classroom doorway, grabbed at the back of her neck and fell to her knees.

A violent wind tore through the broken windows with incredible force. The wind picked up papers and books and other small objects and hurled them through the air. Mattie felt the wind swirling around her with such force that it felt like it might suck the air right out of her lungs.

Something hard struck Mattie's forehead. She closed her eyes and threw an arm over her face. Blindly she reached out. "HENRY!" she screamed at the top of her lungs. Where was he? Then Mattie felt a hand grab her outstretched one. She opened her eyes. It was her brother. Even in the darkness she could see that his eyes were wide with terror. He yanked Mattie toward him and together they crouched down close to the stairwell railing and held on to each other tightly.

"Mattie! What's happening?" Henry shouted.

"I don't know!" Mattie shouted back. "But don't let go of my hand! No matter what happens!"

Mattie pressed herself against the wooden slats of the railing. She could feel the whole building shudder and tremble as the wind beat furiously against the school. Children all around her were crouched in terror, crying and screaming. Then, above the sound of the wind and the screams of the students, Mattie heard a new sound—a deep, dull roar. At first the roar seemed to be coming from far away. But it quickly grew louder and louder. It sounded like a huge freight train bearing down on them.

Mattie was more afraid than she'd ever been in her life. She squeezed Henry's hand with all her might. Her mouth was open and she knew she was screaming. But she couldn't hear her own voice. The sound of it was drowned out completely by the growling, grinding, deafening roar of the storm.

A sudden hard jolt shook the entire building as something gave way on the main floor. Boards buckled and snapped. Mattie felt the floor beneath her tilt down. In the same instant, the wall at the end of the hallway collapsed. Plaster, bricks, and boards were suddenly flying through the air.

Mattie felt herself start to slide down the slanting floorboards toward the jagged open space in the wall ahead of her. She felt Henry's grip tighten like a vise on her hand. He pulled so hard her arm felt like it was going to tear out of its socket. Mattie frantically clawed at the floor with her free hand and kicked with her feet, trying desperately to climb back up and away from the hole in the wall. The wind was screaming around her, tugging at her clothes. She knew if Henry let go, she would be sucked out and away.

But Henry didn't let go. Mattie lay there on the slanting floor, aware of screaming children sliding past her. She gripped Henry's hand and hung on for dear life.

Beyond the hole in the wall, the world had turned into a whirling, swirling nightmare. A black churning mass of wind and dirt and flying objects. Mattie saw entire trees, part of a rooftop, a wagon wheel, and what might have been a person soar past.

Mattie closed her eyes and squeezed them tightly shut. She was sure that she was going to die. Henry couldn't hold on forever. All other thoughts were driven from her mind by the roar of the wind.

She felt that any second she was going to be sucked outside into the whirling nightmare of the black cloud.

Then, almost as quickly as it had started, the frightful roaring began to die down. The wind subsided. In less than a minute, it had stopped completely. Outside it began to rain, a drenching downpour. The only thing that Mattie could hear above the drumming of the rain on the roof was the sound of children sobbing.

# CHAPTER 4

# After the Storm

MATTIE OPENED HER EYES. She blinked as light poured in from the gaping hole in the side of the school where the wall had collapsed. It was suddenly silent and the sky outside was brightening.

Henry shifted his grip slightly and pulled. "Come on, Mattie!" he cried. "Grab on here!"

Mattie clawed and kicked her way toward her brother and the stairwell railing that he was clutching with his other hand. The fingers of her free hand curled around something solid, and she pulled herself up beside her brother. The floor here was still level. But beyond it, where Mattie had been, it was slanting steeply down.

"Are you OK?" she asked her brother.

Henry nodded. A thin trickle of blood was making its way down his face from a cut on his forehead. Mattie looked him over carefully. Other than the cut on his face, Henry seemed unhurt.

Close by, someone groaned. Up and down the hallway, children were beginning to move. Some were sobbing. Some were silent, too stunned or too scared to make a sound. Many were cut and bleeding. Several appeared to have broken arms or legs.

Mattie noticed Mrs. Patterson sitting up against the hallway wall a few feet from them. She was very pale. Her clothes were covered in blood.

Mattie heard the principal's voice. He and several other teachers were making their way up the stairs, which were littered with broken glass. When they reached the top of the stairs they stared at the gaping hole in the wall. Working together, the adults managed to rescue three children who were still clinging desperately to the slanted floor, poised to slide down and out.

The principal tried to sound calm when he said in a loud voice: "Those of you who can walk, go downstairs! Go outside! Go home! We'll help those who are hurt."

Henry struggled to his feet, pulling Mattie up with him. Her legs were weak. Shakily they headed for the top of the stairs. When they passed Mrs. Patterson, Mattie bent down and put her hand on her teacher's arm. Mrs. Patterson licked her lips and then spoke in a voice so soft and low it was barely a whisper. "It's OK, Mattie. They'll help me."

Reluctantly, Mattie stood up and followed her brother. They stepped over some wooden beams that had fallen out of the ceiling. Pinned beneath them—and motionless— were two children from Henry's class. Mattie stepped past them quickly, feeling sick inside. She and Henry crept down the stairs.

The first floor of the school was in ruins. Glass, plaster, books, and bits of furniture were everywhere. Stunned, bleeding children were moving slowly toward the front door. Someone's panicked mother was making her way against the flow, calling out "Mary! Mary!"

Mattie and Henry stumbled out the front door and down the steps of the school. It had stopped raining and now everything was eerily silent and still.

Out in the schoolyard they stopped, staring in disbelief at what had happened to their once familiar world. The schoolyard looked liked it had been swept clean by some giant's great broom. Several of the big trees were gone, simply whisked away. Others were lying uprooted across the ground.

Looking back, Mattie could see that one corner of the school building had collapsed and parts of the walls there had fallen away. Many of the windows in the school had been blown out.

"Was it a tornado, Mattie?" Henry asked.

"I think so," Mattie answered. "It must have been. But I didn't see a **funnel cloud.**"

The houses that had been across the street minutes before were now little more than piles of broken boards jumbled together like so many matchsticks. As Mattie stared at the rubble, a terrible fear boiled up inside her. Were her parents all right? What had happened at the farm?

"We need to get home," Mattie said to her brother. From the look on Henry's face, he had been thinking about their parents too. Together they turned and started walking toward Walnut Street, the road out of town.

As far as they could see in every direction, there wasn't a full house standing. Most were in ruins. Others had been completely swept away. Only their concrete foundations were left to show where the houses had been.

The streets were littered with crumpled automobiles, pieces of furniture, timbers, sheets of tin, street signs, concrete blocks, shingles, bedding, and other **debris.** As Mattie and Henry turned a corner, they saw fallen telegraph and electricity poles lying across their path. They started to walk toward them when a man suddenly

---

**funnel cloud** – a cone-shaped cloud that projects from the base of a thundercloud
**debris** – the remains of something broken down or destroyed

started shouting. "Watch out for the wires! The live wires!" he cried, motioning them away.

People were beginning to emerge from the ruins. Mattie and Henry watched several people crawl out from partially collapsed buildings. They saw a man climb out of a basement—all the rest of his house was gone. They passed people standing in front of what had been their houses, or stores, or offices. Many simply stood in stunned silence, not yet able to take in what had happened. Others sobbed or cried or moaned. One woman screamed hysterically as she held an injured child in her arms.

Dozens of injured people were lying among the ruins. Many were bleeding. There were bodies, too, which Mattie and Henry hurried past.

Mattie and Henry kept walking, stepping around or climbing over obstacles in the streets. Eventually they reached a crossroads and struck out down the main street. Mattie stopped once to look back. Scattered fires had broken out around what was left of Murphysboro. Smoke from the fires curled slowly into the sky where the clouds were breaking up, revealing patches of blue sky. The sun came out and shone down brightly on the ruined town.

Momentarily confused, Mattie and Henry stood still, not daring to move. Then Henry spotted the downed electrical wires lying in a tangled heap on the ground several yards away. They were live, still snapping and crackling. As they backed away, Mattie saw a man lying beneath the tangle, his body crushed and burned.

The main street was nearly unrecognizable. The concrete sidewalks had been torn out of the ground. Almost nothing remained of the stores and offices. Mattie stopped briefly and stared at what was left of Blakewell's Dress Shop. It was just a pile of bricks, rubble, and shattered glass. She spotted a torn piece of red fabric

snagged on a brick that might have been part of a dress, and a single leather shoe. Everything else was gone.

Mattie had hoped the tornado had disappeared after it left Murphysboro. But as she and her brother walked out of town, they could see that the tornado had kept right on going. In the countryside, grass had been torn from the ground. Fields were scoured of topsoil. The trees along the road were stripped of all their leaves and branches. They looked like flagpoles jammed into the

ground. Some of the largest trees had been split or uprooted and now lay like broken bones across the road.

As they passed one of the fallen trees, Henry stopped and simply pointed. Mattie looked and gasped. A fence post had been driven straight through the tree trunk—like a knife into butter—with part of it sticking out on either side. Mattie shuddered at the incredible force needed to do something like that.

Both Mattie and Henry were cold. A chill wind had sprung up. It was pushing puffy white clouds hurriedly across the sky. "Come on," Mattie said, tugging at her brother's sleeve. "We've got to keep moving."

Soon they passed a farm that was just a mile from their own. It was devastated. The barn was smashed and the house was gone. Horses and cattle lay crippled and dying in the pastures. Mattie couldn't bear the sounds the injured animals made. She covered her ears as they ran by.

When they reached the big bend in the road, Mattie's heart began to pound. Had the tornado turned here too and destroyed their farm? Or had it kept going straight and missed it? She and Henry started to walk faster. They broke into a run.

Up ahead was their farm. Mattie couldn't see the top of the windmill above the trees. It was gone. She felt panic rising in her throat. She could see the drive. Henry reached it first and turned off the road. Mattie was right behind him. Gasping for breath, she stopped. The windmill was lying across the farmyard broken into pieces. But the barn was still standing. And so was the house.

Henry had reached the gate. "Mother! Father!" he shouted as he ran toward the porch.

The screen door slammed, and Stella Dunn came leaping down the porch steps. She hugged Henry and reached out for her daughter. Mattie nearly collapsed in her arms.

"Oh, thank goodness," she whispered, holding on to them tightly.

Mattie heard footsteps crunching on the gravel behind them. Seconds later she felt her father's arms close around her, encircling all of them. For the first time since the black cloud had formed on the horizon that afternoon, Mattie felt safe.

Stella ran her hand gently over Henry's forehead. "Henry, you're hurt!"

"Nah, it's nothing," he replied. "Just a cut."

Mattie looked up at her parents. "Did you see the tornado?"

Her father shook his head. "Believe it or not," he began, "I was down in the storm cellar, working on the doors. Suddenly I heard your mother shouting."

Stella picked up the story. "I saw the black cloud from the house. I ran out to warn your father. By the time I got there, the cloud was very close and the wind started to howl. I've never seen anything move so fast."

"We leaped into the cellar," her father went on, "slammed the doors and bolted them. I'd fixed all but one of the hinges. Still, when the tornado hit, I was afraid the doors might be torn away and that we'd be sucked out by the wind. But the doors held. In a few minutes, it was all over." He paused. "I think we were at the edge of the storm, really. If it had passed right over us, I think we'd both be dead."

Mattie hugged her father, burying her face in his chest. He gently tilted her head up with his hand and looked into her face. "Mattie, what happened in town? Is there a lot of damage?"

Mattie swallowed hard. "The tornado went right through Murphysboro. It hit our school. Most of the town is destroyed."

Mattie and Henry told their parents the story as they sat in the kitchen sipping hot tea. Stella and William listened in horrified silence.

Mattie's father was the first to speak. "Sounds like lots of people have been injured. They'll be needing all the help they can get in Murphysboro." He stood up, and reached for his jacket by the door.

A horse's hooves clattered on the gravel outside. Mattie's mother rushed to the window and looked out.

A carriage was coming up the drive. "It's Alice Calder," she said, hurrying to the door. The Calders were a young couple who lived about two miles from the Dunns.

Mattie followed Henry and her parents outside. "Help me, please!" shouted Mrs. Calder, reining the horse in and jumping down from the wagon. "Albert's been hurt." She looked back into the wagon. There lay her husband, barely conscious. His face and hands were covered with bruises and cuts.

"When the twister hit," Mrs. Calder said breathlessly, "Albert was running for the house. But halfway across the yard, the wind picked him up. He looked as though he were flying for a few seconds. Then he hit the ground hard and tumbled over and over. When I got to him, he

was unconscious. It was all I could do to get him into the wagon." She paused to catch her breath. "Yours is the first place I found that wasn't completely gone. Please, can you help him?"

Stella put her arm around the young woman. "You calm yourself, Alice. We'll get him inside." She turned to Mattie. "Honey, go in and clear off the kitchen table. We'll put him there so I can dress these wounds."

Mattie's father and Henry carried the young farmer into the kitchen. When they laid him on the kitchen table, his eyelids fluttered and he groaned softly.

"Henry, start boiling some water. Mattie, run upstairs and get some clean sheets and the ointments from the medicine cabinet." Stella gave out orders as she examined Mr. Calder's head.

When Mattie returned, her mother was cleaning the cuts on Mr. Calder's face. Henry was pouring water into a big kettle on the stove. Her father was watching the whole scene with a thoughtful look on his face.

After a moment he spoke. "Stella, I've got to get into Murphysboro and see how I can help. But if ours is the only undamaged house in the area, I expect there will be other people coming here, looking for help and shelter. Will you be all right here?"

"We'll be fine," said Mattie's mother without looking up from what she was doing.

"Henry," William said, turning to his son. "I want you to stay here with your mother." Henry started to protest, but his father interrupted quickly. "We need a man at the house while I am gone. We don't know who might show up here. Henry, I'm putting you in charge, OK?"

Henry's angry look turned to one of pride as he realized the responsibility his father had just given him.

"Mattie," said her father, turning to her. "Are you up to coming with me, to going back into Murphysboro?"

Mattie thought of the damage and the dead bodies. The idea of going back was scary. But she wanted to help. She looked at her father and nodded.

"OK, then let's go hitch Charger up to the wagon," he said, heading for the door. "Mrs. Calder's horse is tired and a little spooked. We'll put him in the barn."

Ten minutes later, Mattie climbed up beside her father in the front of the wagon. He flicked the reins on Charger's back, and they sped down the road in the late afternoon sun. Ahead in the distance, plumes of dark smoke hung like shadows above Murphysboro.

# CHAPTER 5

# Recovery

MATTIE AND WILLIAM quickly reached Murphysboro. There was much more activity in the town now than when Mattie had seen it last. People who had not been injured had rushed in to help those who were hurt.

Some of the downed trees and telegraph poles that had been blocking the streets had been pulled out of the way so wagons could pass. Mattie and her father drove toward Main Street.

"This is unbelievable!" Mattie's father said, shaking his head as he tried to take in all the destruction. "Looks like a big steam roller came through and smashed everything." In the distance, they heard the wail of a train whistle. "Sounds like the trains are running," he added. "That's good news."

A man was hurrying toward them, waving his arms. "Hey, Mister," he shouted. "We could sure use your

help." He came running up beside them. "And your
wagon," he added breathlessly.

"Hop in," said Mattie's father. "How can we help?"

The man pulled himself up into the wagon. He
pointed down the street. "See that clearing down there?
There are injured people there that need to be taken to

the depot. They've put up a hospital tent there. The worst cases are going to Carbondale by train."

William snapped the reins and the wagon lurched. As they headed down the street, William asked, "How long have the trains been running?"

"Soon as word got out about the tornado and how bad it was," answered the man.

"How bad was it?" Mattie asked.

"Well, news is coming along in bits and pieces, with the people who are coming in to help," the man said. "Not sure of all the details yet. But the tornado—or whatever it was—apparently started in Missouri early this afternoon. From there it headed northeast. Then it moved through five counties in Missouri and then crossed the Mississippi. It hit Gorham about 2:30. They say several dozen people are dead there, and the town is pretty much destroyed. About ten minutes after that, the twister hit Murphysboro."

"Any idea how many people were hurt here?" asked Mattie's father.

"Well, they keep finding more all the time," the man said, sighing. "Hundreds, easily. Maybe hundreds dead, too. We won't know for a while. People are buried under stuff, and missing. Worst thing I've ever seen."

Hundreds dead? Mattie felt cold inside. She realized just how incredibly lucky she and her family had been.

The man went on. "The Red Cross nurse who is helping here said the tornado didn't stop at Murphysboro. Seems it kept right on going across southern Illinois and on into Indiana." The man pointed ahead. "Stop right up here," he said. Then he jumped down as the wagon came to a stop. Mattie's father jumped down and handed Charger's reins over to her.

Several badly injured people were on blankets on the ground. Mattie had never seen such terrible wounds. A young dark-haired woman with a white cap was bending over one of them. Mattie guessed she was the Red Cross nurse the man had mentioned. She was tying a sling around a man's arm. He groaned in pain as she carefully positioned his arm in the sling.

"Now try not to move," she said, glancing over at the Dunn's wagon. "It looks as though help is here. Now we'll be able to get you to a doctor as soon as possible to set your broken arm."

The nurse stood up and came over to Mattie's father. She explained how the injured people should be carried and which ones should be taken first. William and the other man nodded and went to work.

The nurse looked up at Mattie as she sat on the wagon. "I could use your help, too."

Mattie tied off the reins and jumped down. The woman pointed to a small barrel on the ground. "There's fresh water in that barrel. You'll find a cup beside it. You can give all these people a drink."

Mattie found the water and cup. One by one, she brought water to the injured people. She had to hold the cup for most of them because they were too weak to hold it themselves. Several of the people whispered, "Thank you." One woman struggled to raise herself up on one arm. She grabbed Mattie's shoulder and searched her face.

"Have you seen my boy? His name's Frankie!" she said, frantically. "He's just three years old. Have you seen my Frankie?"

Mattie said she hadn't seen Frankie, but that people were searching for survivors. She tried to be encouraging. But it didn't seem to help. The woman lay back down, muttering her son's name over and over again.

When the wagon was full, Mattie hopped up beside her father. He drove slowly along the streets, weaving his way around piles of rubble. At the train station, the injured people were carried into a tent where several doctors and nurses were working. The Salvation Army was there too.

Mattie and her father learned that the Illinois Central Railroad had sent the first relief train to Murphysboro, carrying medical people and supplies. Since then, the train had been traveling back and forth between Murphysboro and the neighboring town of Carbondale. The train was taking injured and homeless people from Murphysboro to Carbondale and bringing back more volunteers and medical supplies.

Uniformed men from the National Guard arrived as well. Mattie saw some of them in the train station, loading medical supplies and food into wagons to be distributed around the town. They were also setting up tents just outside Murphysboro for people who had been left homeless by the storm.

Mattie and her father worked into the night. They brought more injured people to the train station. They helped deliver boxes of food and stacks of blankets to relief stations around town. There was no electricity in Murphysboro. After the sun went down, people worked by the light of kerosene lanterns.

Around midnight, Mattie and her father had just delivered several more people to the train station. William climbed into the seat beside his daughter. As he took the reins, he looked down at Mattie and noticed the dark circles under her eyes. Her shoulders sagged from exhaustion.

"I think we should go home, Mattie," William said gently. "It's been a terrible day. And I think we should get back to Henry and your mother."

"But shouldn't we keep helping?" Mattie asked, looking out into the dark shadows around them.

"We've helped a lot," her father answered. "And there are many more people here than when we arrived. Help is coming from all over. Besides, we don't know what kind of help your mother and Henry are needing back at the house right now."

Mattie thought for a moment. "OK," she said. "But I think we should come back again tomorrow."

"Absolutely," her father said, nodding. He flicked the reins and Charger leaned into his harness. The wagon rumbled slowly out of Murphysboro and into the inky darkness of the countryside.

Wearily, Mattie leaned against her father, comforted by the strong, solid feeling of his shoulder. What if something had happened to him or to her mother? What if she and Henry had come back to the farm to find both of them badly injured or dead? Just thinking about the possibility made Mattie start to shake.

Mattie's father felt her shiver. He put his arm around her and pulled her close.

When they reached the bend in the road, Mattie straightened up. She peered into the darkness, anxious to catch the first glimpse of home. Charger sensed they were nearing home and started to trot a little faster.

Lights appeared through the trees in the grove. They turned off the road and started up the drive. Coming toward them was another wagon. Mattie's father pulled back on the reins, bringing Charger to a stop. "Hello. Who's there?" he called out.

The other wagon slowly drew up beside them. The big bearded man holding the reins wore a National Guardsman's cap.

"Evening, sir," he said. "I'm Lieutenant Hicks, sir, National Guard." The man saluted. "Is this your house?"

William nodded. "What's going on?"

"Just delivering a few more tornado survivors, sir," the lieutenant replied. "Your house is one of the few still standing this close to Murphysboro." He paused, shifting in his seat. "I'll probably be bringing in a few more from town tonight. They've no place else to go. Some are injured." He paused. "But there's an amazing woman in there looking after them all."

"That would be my wife," William replied. Mattie smiled proudly to herself. Of course her mother was taking care of everyone!

The soldier saluted again and flicked the reins. Mattie turned and watched the wagon disappear into the darkness. "Come on, Mattie," her father said, urging Charger forward. "Let's go see how your mother and Henry are doing."

When they got to the house, a woman and her young son were sitting huddled together on the porch, wrapped in a blanket. The woman's head was bandaged. The boy looked frightened. The woman nodded at them politely.

Inside the house were other strangers. A man with his leg in a splint lay sleeping on the couch in the parlor. There were people sitting in all of the chairs. A young couple sat by the fire, sipping cups of coffee.

Henry came down the stairs. He had a blanket tucked under each of his arms. When he saw Mattie and his father, he ran over to them. William threw an arm around his son's shoulders.

"Obviously you have everything under control," he said looking down proudly at his son.

"A lot has happened since you left," Henry said.

"Tell us in a minute," William replied. "First, where's your mother?"

"In the kitchen," Henry answered.

William and Mattie headed for the kitchen. Mattie could hear her mother's voice. When she reached the doorway, she saw her mother kneeling beside a girl with long, mud-caked hair. The girl was sitting in a chair by the table with her back to Mattie. Stella held the girl's hand in one of hers. With a damp cloth she was gently wiping dirt and blood off the girl's arm. "Almost done,"

she was saying to the girl, very gently and quietly. "And then we'll get you out of your dirty clothes and into something fresh."

Stella looked up at her daughter and husband standing in the kitchen doorway. Seeing the rest of her family safe, she gave a smile of relief. Stella laid the girl's arm down carefully in her lap and stood up.

"Mattie," she said beckoning to her daughter. "Here's someone you know from school who needs our help."

Mattie walked over to her mother. She turned toward the girl in the chair and found herself looking into the face of Amanda Blakewell.

"Amanda!" Mattie blurted out. She hardly recognized her tormentor. Amanda's hair hung limply in dark, dirty strands. The beautiful dress she'd been wearing that morning, the one with the white sash, was the color of mud. It was wet and torn. Amanda's arms and legs and face were covered with deep cuts. Mattie remembered how the glass from the windows had flown through the air when the tornado had hit the school.

Amanda didn't say a word. It took Mattie a few seconds to realize that Amanda seemed to be looking off into the distance. "Amanda?" Mattie said questioningly. Again, Amanda didn't reply.

"Yes, it's Amanda Blakewell," said Mattie's mother, still speaking very softly. She drew her daughter slightly away from the girl in the chair. "Mattie," her mother started in a low voice, "Amanda was just brought out here from town. Both her parents were killed. Their house and store collapsed, and they didn't get out alive." Mattie's mother paused. "Amanda's clothes are wet and filthy. Why don't you take her upstairs and help her change into something of yours. I think she's about your size."

Mattie swallowed hard. When she had first seen Amanda's face, anger had bubbled up inside her. The person she disliked most in the world was sitting at her kitchen table, and her mother was being so kind to her! All of Amanda's cruel words came flooding back. The sound of her mocking voice echoed in Mattie's head. She stood there, too stunned to move.

Mattie finally looked up at her mother. Should she tell her mother how terrible Amanda had been to her over the past few weeks? Should she try to explain why Amanda Blakewell didn't deserve any help—especially from Mattie?

Stella Dunn looked searchingly at her daughter, a slight frown on her face. "Mattie?" she repeated. "Will you take Amanda upstairs, please?"

Mattie looked from her mother to her father. On the ride home from Murphysboro, she'd thought how awful it would have been to lose her parents. The pain she felt just thinking about losing them had been unbearable.

How much more would it hurt if she had really lost her parents—like Amanda had?

She looked back at Amanda again. The girl with the china-blue eyes was still staring off into space.

"Yes," Mattie said at last. "Yes, I will." She walked over to Amanda and stretched out her hand. "Come on, Amanda. Let's go up to my room."

Wordlessly, Amanda took her hand. She stood up and let Mattie lead her out of the kitchen and up the wooden steps to Mattie's bedroom.

"You sit here," Mattie said, patting the foot of the bed. Amanda sat down.

Mattie went over to her wardrobe and opened the door. She looked at the dresses hanging there for a long time. She reached up and fingered the worn fabric of the brown dress that she'd worn to school the day before, the one with the mended tear that Amanda had made fun of. Then Mattie pushed it aside. She reached for the

dress that was hanging next to it, the yellow one with the cream-colored lace.

Mattie brought the dress over to Amanda and laid it on the bed beside her. For the first time, Amanda responded. She reached out and touched the dress, smoothing the crisp fabric. "It's pretty," she whispered.

Surprised, Mattie didn't say anything for a few seconds. But when she answered, there was a strange new confidence in her voice.

"Yes, it is, Amanda. And it'll look real nice on you."

# The Tri-State Tornado of 1925

▲ Logan School before and after the Tri-State Tornado

 JUST AFTER 1 A.M. on March 18, 1925, a tornado descended from the sky northwest of Ellington, Missouri. During the next three hours, more people died and more buildings were destroyed than from any other tornado in American history. The tornado reached between a half mile to a mile wide and left a path of destruction across three states. It finally broke up around 4:30 p.m. near Petersburg, Indiana. The Tri-State Tornado had traveled from Missouri to Illinois to Indiana.

In its wake, the tornado left a path of destruction 216 miles long. There were 695 people dead, and more than 2,000 injured. Several towns in the tornado's path were completely destroyed, including Annapolis, Missouri; Gorham, Illinois; Parrish, Illinois; and Griffin, Indiana.

## An Unusual Storm

The Tri-State Tornado was an unusual storm. Traveling at an average speed of 63 miles per hour, it was one of the fastest tornadoes on record. As it moved from Gorham, Illinois, into Murphysboro, it was traveling at a speed of about 73 miles per hour. This is more than twice as fast as a typical tornado.

The Tri-State Tornado didn't look like a normal tornado, either. Most eyewitnesses did not see a funnel cloud, the characteristic coil of whirling, snaking wind that descends from the sky like a deadly finger. They mostly recalled seeing an enormous dark cloud in the southwestern sky. It was very low to the ground and moving toward them very fast. As a result, most people did not recognize that the storm was a tornado until it was too late to escape its deadly power.

## Destruction in Murphysboro

Murphysboro suffered the greatest losses. The 234 deaths that were reported included 25 from three different schools in the town. The schools were built of brick. Most of the children who died in the schools were killed when walls collapsed on top of them.

Much of the town of Murphysboro was devastated by the tornado. Many homes were completely destroyed, leaving almost half of the town's population homeless. Many of those homeless people lived in tent camps set up by the National Guard. Others were taken in by families whose homes had survived the tornado.

Telephone lines were down all along the tornado's path. News of the disaster reached the outside world by radio. When people did learn what had happened, help came swiftly from nearby states. Eventually help arrived from all over the country. The Red Cross and the Salvation Army sent

▼ **One of the Open-Air Emergency Aid Stations that helped homeless people after the tornado disaster**

doctors, nurses, and teams of volunteers. Medicine, food, and clothing for the tornado victims was also sent.

In 1925, there was no such thing as a tornado warning system. There was no way to alert people to take shelter from an approaching storm. Today, tornado warning systems have helped to reduce the number of deaths that occur from tornadoes.

## Understanding Tornadoes

Tornadoes are extremely dangerous storms. A tornado is a giant whirlwind that is created by severe, rotating thunderstorm clouds called supercells. Tornadoes typically occur in the spring or summer when the air is warm. If a storm pushes cooler air into a warm area, the warm air is forced up quickly. This movement of air can cause stormy and windy conditions.

Sometimes the storm winds begin to move in a circular pattern. These winds can pick up speed and form a funnel cloud. If a funnel cloud touches down on Earth, it can move along the ground, destroying everything in its path. As the funnel cloud moves, it can also pick up and throw around debris. The injuries and deaths that occur during a tornado are often caused by this fast-moving debris.

▼ **This F4 tornado in Oklahoma was later classified as F5.**

# How a Tornado Works

1. Tornadoes begin inside a huge thundercloud.

2. Warm air, close to the ground, rises quickly and creates a funnel of spinning air.

3. Cooler air descends into the funnel of spinning air. Then this air warms and rises.

4. If the funnel cloud touches the ground, it is called a tornado.

## Predicting Tornadoes

In 1948, the first tornado forecast was issued by the Air Force at Tinker Air Force Base in Oklahoma. Government weather forecasters started issuing tornado watches in 1952. In the 1950s, weather radar was developed and tracking tornadoes became easier and warnings were more accurate.

Today, a network of weather-warning radio stations, storm-tracking radar systems, and satellites make it possible for forecasters to issue tornado alerts that give people precious time to flee a tornado or take cover before it hits.

Over time, weather forecasters developed a scale to measure the destructive power of tornadoes. The Fujita Scale ranks tornadoes according to their estimated wind speed. The most destructive tornadoes are classified as F5 on the Fujita Scale, F5 tornadoes have estimated wind speed of between 261 and 318 miles per hour. Based on the amount of destruction and the reports of eyewitnesses, meteorologists believe the Tri-State Tornado was an F5.

On average, about 1,000 tornadoes are recorded in the United States every year. That's more than any other country in the world. A large number of those tornadoes occur in the states of Nebraska, Iowa, Kansas, Oklahoma, and Texas. This group of states have been the nickname "Tornado Alley."

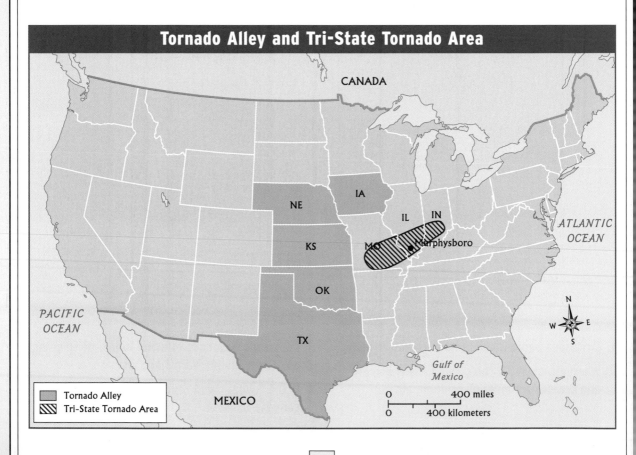

**Tornado Alley and Tri-State Tornado Area**

# Write an Eyewitness Account

THE TORNADO in Murphysboro changed the lives of the people living there. Throughout history there have been many other tornadoes that have caused damage and destruction to the areas where they happened.

- Choose a tornado that has occurred in the past.

- Research the effects of the tornado on the land and the people who lived near this tornado.

- Write questions to guide your research. Then write the related information you find on note cards.

- Use the information you gather to write an eyewitness account of the tornado. Write as if you were someone who witnessed the tornado.

Did you know the tornado was going to happen?

How did you feel during the tornado?

What did you do to prepare for the tornado?

What type of damage did the tornado cause?

# Read More About Tornadoes

FIND AND READ more books about tornadoes. As you read, think about these questions. They will help you understand more about this topic.

- What are some of the causes of tornadoes?

- Can you name some of the major tornadoes in history?

- Can scientists predict when a tornado will occur? What instruments do they use?

- Where do tornadoes normally occur? Why do they occur in these places?

- Why are tornadoes dangerous?

**SUGGESTED READING**
**Reading Expeditions**
*Earth Science:*
*Extreme Weather*

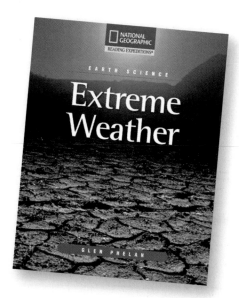